An Anthology

By Terrance J. Scott Jr.

Proverbs 18:21- "The tongue has the power of life & death, and those who love it will eat its fruit."

I dedicate this to my Creator, my family, my past, and my future......

Also, this one's for "You"…..you know who you are…..

Cover Design: Brittany Janay Jackson

Published by G Publishing, LLC
P. O. Box 24374
Detroit, MI 48224

ISBN 13: 978-0-9801297-9-3
      10: 0-9801297-9-6

Library of Congress Control Number: 2007910351

Printed in the United States of America

About the Author

Terrance J. Scott Jr. was born January 14, 1991 in Detroit, MI. Since he was small child, he has always enjoyed music. When BET's "The Box" was a popular show, family members and friends have videotaped him and watched in awe as a toddler recited lines from Tupac, Notorious B.I.G., Rakim, etc. His love for music and poetry never escaped him. As time passed, in fact, he grew and matured in music, as did his lyrics. Common, Kanye West, Mos Def, Lupe Fiasco, Nas, Alicia Keys, and Lauren Hill became some of his favorites because their music was strictly poetry laced with instruments and talent, which is what Rap (Rhythm & Poetry) and R&B (Rhythm and Blues) are supposed to be. In that he considers himself a poet and not a rapper, because today's rap has a plethora of negative connotations to which he chooses to disassociate himself from. Terrance's poetry talks about more than money, sex, guns, drugs, the ghetto, and dancing to soup and candy. To him, poetry has a meaning and is thus meaningful. This notion stemmed the title "Divine Intervention", simply another term for a miracle, because it describes poetry and, in essence, even enhances it.

Introduction

I still plan to pursue a career in the technological,

It's just I've realized my power to be melodical

Look at the fact that I can overcome my obstacles

Through the Power of Poetry I didn't know was so powerful

You can say what you want, proper grammar is optional,

Unlimited metaphors, running out is impossible,

Like I don't wear glasses, I wear "opticals",

Or I don't write poems, I write chronicles….

I'm grateful for this gift, *un*like the Son that was Prodigal,

It's semi-logical, and it makes you feel unstoppable

Like if I step on the court, I know Kobe is rockable,

And if Shaq steps up, I'm confident that he's droppable!

Some of the things I'm saying shouldn't be much of a shock to you

If they are, I promise you that this isn't diabolical

The chance of you disagreeing with me is probable,

But the fact that I don't care means that you have a lot to do......

Welcome......to my world........my miracle.........Divine Intervention......

Table of Contents

Love and Recognition

Ode to Poetry

My poetry is the possibility of language,

It's like a friend you can hang with,

When I desire to inquire more than I can say,

Like the stove as opposed to the microwave,

You want things done right in the nicest way,

So don't say nothing if you have nothing nice to say....

Poetry is an emotion that alters a person's motion,

And it exists within you, yet it's very outspoken....

Painful memories inside constantly murmuring,

It disappears in your sleep like surgery,

It burns in your mind like mouthwash gurgling,

Then runs down your body like you've been hurdling.

Finally, when you feel like you're going to bust,

You turn to the one that you know you can trust.

It doesn't snitch on you and it gives you a rush,

That helps you write 16 bars and not cuss.

Just when you think it's over, you're not done yet,

So keep jogging because you don't need to run yet.

What's wrong?

      You mad?

            Not having fun yet?

Ask yourself these same questions, smile, and take one guess…

Some people might find that to be absurd,

The truth is a poet speaks unlimited words

I can write and go on for years,

But you can't see sound so how do you know that I'm even here………

Ode to Mama

To my beginning, like birth

God created the Heavens and the Earth

After making Adam, He performed a procedure like no other

He took one of his ribs and thus formed the mother

Mother, the basis of all life

The one that comes to my side and makes things alright.

Through sickness and health, poverty and wealth,

Mama always seems to be there when you need her help

So stop running when you see her belt,

She does it out of love despite what you've seen or felt,

She's not always going to be seen like stealth

So don't laugh if she coughs after she sneezed then belched!

Mama thank you for all that you've done,

Because if you didn't keep me in church I wouldn't know I was God's son.

So as I move on in life through obstacles and drama,

I can look back and find time to give thanks to my Mama....

Ode to Dad

To my Dad, my introduction

The one who introduced me to the power of love with abduction.

See while you abducted me into the videogame world and electricity,

You showed me life past simplicity.

We have a lot in common, but also a lot of common differences,

Time that we've shared and time that remains mischievous…….

There's been some close calls, and some distances…..

But everyone who knows me are all eyewitnesses

To the fact that I'm a man because a man was a man and this man showed me how I supposed to be a man

Agreement, not always, on either side,

This has been a tough, "emotional rollercoaster" ride….

But the past is the past, what's done is done

We've had a bittersweet time like Coke and Rum

So to my Tekken Master that still hasn't beaten Final Fantasy!

I hope I've been a son that is your Final Fantasy

Time to move forward

Ode to Sis

To my most adorable and precious gift,

The one who keeps my brain soaked and wet like the
"Maid of the Mist"

Because of you all the blood has rushed to my mind,

My headache from laughs or irritation through time

We've grown, cried, lied, laughed, and have been mean
to each other

But I swear I would trade you for no other

At times you're a hang-nail, but mostly you're my soul

I never thought I'd see us grow old…..

From you cheerleading me in basketball,

To Granddaddy's basement playing "Roller Ball"

I haven't been the nicest, you haven't shown the most dexterity,

We have an odd relationship like hairy knees!

But I love you with all my heart,

Stay my Lisa, and I'll always be your Bart

Ode to High School

High school, a fresh start, a new chance,

To be the best, a Legend like Bagger Vance

Hoping to succeed and be on top of my game,

While I had a misconception of the experience I'd gain.

At first I was fearful, afraid of the change;

Unsure if I was ready to grow like grain

I mean I already felt like a tumbleweed compared to
daisies

Inadequacy hastened my long to be a Ghost like Swayze

Looking like a pistachio in Candy Land,

Dressed like Celie entering a fashion show

I had a Clue that being Blue wasn't Handy-Dandy man,

So I brushed my shoulders and turned this salt into
cookie dough

Gained associates, put some time in

Experimented with amateur, low-dose rhyming

And wasn't focused on my grades

A 14 year old trying to get laid......

I speak the truth, no lies

I had to go through that to be the man that I am today

Everyone who was a teen can relate

I was a goofball searching for a new me

Jumping day to day from class clown to cool breeze

Sophomore year, I had to change lanes

I realized what I wanted, and had a scholarship to maintain

So I pressed on like an iron, and got into a groove

Because this money I simply just couldn't lose

Speaking of losing I became extremely tired of being fat

It relentlessly irked my nerves like a gnat

So I slimmed down and stretched up, new self-esteem

Once was down, now up, you know what I mean

By Junior Year, my eyes were outstretched

God's blessings had left me perplexed; I wanted to know what was next!

So I began to seek Him and His Holy Spirit

And January 25, 2007, He manifested His Holy Spirit, in me

I gained insight on new things

And began to pursue and confront my new dreams

It began with "*You*", along with acting and writing,

Now speaking up, and speaking out, no more crying and whining

I'm a man now, with a backbone and friends-

      -People that I know have my back until the end

"*You*" and I have grown, apart and mended

Along the way, I made mistakes, and repented

Now I'm a senior, with an urge to stay clean like a dentist

And count my blessings like the Census

Graduation is approaching, and I need all "Life-Coaching", to prep me for the life ahead

I have grown and evolved *unlike* an ape, so thank you for giving me these days, my daily bread

It's been fun…..

Ode to Life's Cousin

I can count heartbeats between my thoughts of you,

You are never too far from my mind.

The very sight of you starts the day off right, like breakfast,

so seeing you is a must like time.

Time tells us how long the Sun will linger in the sky,

but you determine how long I smile.

I've never in my life felt this way before,

and don't know if I will for a while.

As the Earth continues its orbit around the Sun,

I, on the other hand, can't seem to fathom

Where this came from, or where it's going,

all I know is now, how random…….

Seeking success and blessings, no room for imperfection,

give thanks to our God above,

For providing me this once in a lifetime chance,

to experience

Love.

Responsibility

My People

I'm feeling blue like the N-A-V-Y,

But I still feel like fighting like the A-R-M-Y,

I worship Jesus not His M-A-R-Y,

And I'm still tempted to do the thing to get a B-A-B-Y.

This is strictly rhetorical, no need for a reply

I'm stuck on the roof, reaching for T-H-E sky

Trying to grow like Wheat and Rye

And get connections like knees and thighs……..

………. I don't know…………..

Its like I'm blind but I can see my eyes,

Be the epitome of pain, then Vitamin E your cries

Smooth it out with Aloe and Shea Butter,

Put your loads on my back,

    Now I scream inside

I'm almost putting my life in park, and letting my
dreaming ride

    You people are like crack, and I fiend for pipes,

    I'm surrounded by wrong with a need for right

Using the cold of the world to heat my mind....

Confidence

I'm tiptoeing, not breathing in a House of Flying Daggers

Making sure I will never again Fall like Niagara

I've found myself………. now what does that include?

I'm amused at the question and from there I should conclude……

But you see, I've realized a miraculous thing

I'm still a Teen with a Dream to have a voice like King,

Now I've recognized this feat, so I'm going to use it,

I just grab a dictionary and let the words choose it……

I don't have to make hip hop, I'll jus make music,

And you don't have to listen to it

Just let it play, stupid

Money is funny, people come and go

But like a weed, you can cut me and I'm STILL GON GROW!

AND YOU CAN IGNORE ME BUT YOU STILL GON KNOW

THAT IM WOKE ETERNALLY SPITTING STILLBORN FLOWS!

You don't have to like this…

Actually, I hope you don't…..

Because you'll want me to delete this and get mad cause I won't.

I'm going to keep being me, no reason to change for others

That's why I use Cheer so you people won't fade my colors

It does get hard at times when you try to bleach me

So I keep lesson plans with me so you can teach me ….

Deep Water

I'm running as fast as I can and going
nowhere………….

I have on my best outfit for people that won't
stare………

But still don't dare making fun of me, its no fair,

>To you,

>The person wasting their breath because I won't
>care.

I'd be wasting time trying to get back at you,

>Revenge,

>Avenging the vengeance of brutes, knocking
>doors off the hinge,

>The stench of depression surrounds people that
>think we might forget them,

Because they can't hear like Tyson victims

You're in deep water if impressive impressions matter most,

Falling into recessive recessions without a boast,

Just try to avoid aggressive aggression by a coast,

Because your inner hurricane will wipe out anything in its path.

The wrath of wisdom conquering, how long will it last?

I laugh, because this doesn't seem to add up like math

The shaft, the end of the stick, what I always seem to have

This crap ends now, furthermore I'm fighting back.......

...But not with weapons, I'm fighting back with words

Because if I used weapons, I would probably be stuck in a hearse.

Besides, quite frankly I find it absurd

To go berserk and leave this Earth early like Levert

Living Water

No man is perfect and pure, like boiling hot water

We all have a little dirt, like mop water

Some are Kool-Aid, sweet but scared and comfy in the closet,

They won't run until you turn on the faucet

Some are morning people, the grass dew

Others condensate and sit there, glass fools

Like fog, they show up and hate to go

And watch those that think they are just normal H2O

It's funny how some think they're worth double the price

Others just try to be hard like ice

Thinking they're glaciers, when really they're lice

There are few that are fruitful and nice

The body is more liquid than solid,

Earth is more water than land

Yes we were made from dirt,

But remember water makes you a man

Just don't drown......

Daily Struggles

What remains in my drained veins is the pain that complains in disdain-

-straining for rain in this drought for change

Don't aim at the First to cause you pain like Cain-

-because you won't be Abel to tame your brain's maintained stains

I'm trying to be real realistically-

-without the depression of being sad sadistically

The fallacy of reality changes these pure impurities,

So you can look at me and view my kind cruelties.

There's no vaccine for poverty

And being a malicious thief's the wrong way to Gain
Green (gangrene) like fake jewelry

It's Reasonable to Doubt my Blueprints will
make a Dynasty,

Because I'm the only one I'm willing to pay the
price to be

If I wasn't who would you replace with me-

-that difficult question makes one face
complacency

Having a revolutionized revelation,

-makes writing these words sweeter, like
celebrating celebrations

Truth Hurts

I know how it feels not to be liked, like Mike Jones

That's why I add a little fight when I write songs

That's why I add a little bite, like a python

So the spice in this recipe will make this quite long

That's why I do what I do, despite what you think of me,

You inspire me and you might get an inkling,

That when I spit, I direct it towards you,

Because I'm still probably hated by most, and loved by few

And don't live for others, but live for yourself,

Live for the Lord and live for your health

Because if you live for the fame and live for the wealth,

You always seem to stumble and fall short

Slip & fall trying to put the ball in my court,

Like not graduating because you can't call on a dork…

I'm talking to everybody of all different sorts

Even those that walk up & down the hall for support

Yea, I'm calling you out, like an "Iso"

But I'm still fighting for life like Terry Shivoh.

I'm speaking the truth and you're begging me to please stop,

Because I make your blood boil, and your ease drop.

Just know that I put my all in each line,

My all in each rhyme, and come out on top each time!

I beg to differ if there's a problem with me, clown

Because it takes more than words to bring me down

We all struggle, from adults to the kids with kids that sell drugs to get dividends.

I recognize your cries with my eyes on the prize,

But we're always criticized with lies, even though we try…….

Despite the hype my people, we're still alive!

Despite the negativity, we will survive!

But don't let your guard down because you feel revived,

You avoided getting killed, but you still can die!

If that's the case, then what's the point of giving birth

That's what you're thinking right, why was I put on the Earth?

Well, you were born with a purpose, for what it's worth;

Mine is to write in ways that make the truth hurt…..

And I will keep doing it until I get better,

Like I'm still hoopin' outside, no matter the weather,

It's called determination, it won't come if you aren't patient,

I'm trying to pass it on, so here's my purpose, don't waste it……..

Miscellaneous

Empty Seat

Let's stride…….

Close your eyes……

Set your differences apart and take this dream for a ride

I know love used to dwell where "empty" now resides

I've made you cry, now let me drink the tears from your eyes

Because those eyes glow with the logo of my dreams

Girl, you are the Michael Jordan of my team

You seem fine without me, but I can't win without you

For you taught me how to win even when I doubted you

Look at how we didn't even begin as friends

And now as mine we unfortunately had to end in sin

I'm lost, walking lightless through Jurassic Park

Baby I've been lifeless since we've been apart

You may not even like this, thinking I'm a retard

But the world is nightless with you, there's no dark

Perfection, you complete me

In essence, I beseech thee

To give me one last chance to be the man who completely

Swept you off your feet and not the boy who made you leave me

Let me take you deeper like a simile….

……*in due time*……

Unspoken Agreement

I have something to say but I don't know how to say it

Because I don't want to mess up and words are nothing
to play with

If I was to be too blunt, I might piss you off

But if I was too nice, it'd be too hard to get you off…

We all want to be free and say what we want,

But the package of liberty comes with those that taunt

To avoid that, and get rid of my stigma,

I'm forced to stick with circumstances and just become
an enigma…..

If I didn't have to, I wouldn't, like a prostitute

But sometimes we got to do what we got to do

You give Kobe the ball, if you want the W

And keep your wife happy if you don't want her to double you

You don't need to prove yourself, as long as you aren't gullible

Like sitting money down and thinking it's untouchable......

These words are between us, our little secret,

But I shouldn't have to say that, like an unspoken agreement......

Approach

Excuse me, I don't mean to cause you any spite,

It seems like I just tripped, fell, & landed in your life,

I want more than just a wave, more than just your name,

Because I'm starting to really dig you, like a grave.

Talk is cheap, some say, so I'm trying to prove it,

Through a series of expressions in the form of music.

I see my opportunity and I'm not going to lose it,

Like Hitler & his near genocide against the Jewish.

I know all of this is hard to fathom at once,

But I'm not a daredevil performing any stunts,

This is me being bold, sincere, & plain honest,

Just trying to find a way to turn you on, like the Amish.

Even though YOU may seem to be, I'm not perfect,

That's why entertaining this conversation is worth it,

I'm hoping you feel the same way that I feel,

Once I get out this mirror and say this to you for real......

Brown Sugar

Sunrise to sunset, dawn to dusk

Is the time you know you have someone you trust

Have you ever heard a such thing as a fear to lust?

Because you don't want to ruin something good, you know you must

Keep your distance, stay focused, and pay attention

Because you don't want to be the one to receive "honorable mention"

Maintaining a close friend is the mission

Because you don't want to leave like Ben Wallace did the Pistons…

You just want a friend that's cool and won't tell all your secrets,

Make you laugh, give advice, and be your best defense,

A shoulder to cry on in a certain time of grievance,

Pray with you when you mess up, and help you repent,

Talk just about anytime on the telephone

If one comes on too strong just tell them no

Through all the laughing, crying, and playing, nobody's getting down

A person can only have so many friends like pounds…..

……*I've already lost too much*………

The Walking Past

Like Richard, anything Pryor to *this* is obsolete

The time is tomorrow, forget last week

If the past dwells today, how can we move forward?

We'll be stuck making sequels like Jason horrors

Let the past be the past, preserve the memories

Scratch that name off the board like Emory

It's like the closer tomorrow appears, the past is stalking fast

To the point where I have to walk past my walking past….

Bad habits, mixed feelings never left me alone

To the point where I affected others, in *their* homes

Too close to grown to think like kids, what's going on?

I guess the best part of letting go is *truly* moving on…….

Now your nose starts to sniff, and your brain starts to itch

The million dollar question is arising, *"What if?"*

But *if* you ejaculate it from your mind now

There'll be nothing to fabricate because you won't know how

Trying to be strong, who knew it'd be this rough

Try to move on but you yourself like abrupt

Intentions interrupt, mind gets corrupt-

- Which is the main thing I thought I could trust....

To stitch things back like sutures,

I apologize to *"You"* and Past, and reserve *"You"* for the future........

Past, you'll always be here until the end,

I just hope we never meet like this again......

Running

Space is all around us, I wonder if that's what I take up,

Sometimes I can't sleep because I'm scared I won't wake up…..

These insecure thoughts run through my head constantly,

I'm running from myself because I'm out to get me!

Everybody tells me to slow down,

Before I get caught by a bull in a Texas Hoedown

Forcing me into a corner, compelling a throw down,

I'm not ready for a fight because I'm scared of being broke down….

Running from disease and running from prison,

Scared to be convicted so I run from religion,

Not ready to be seen so I run from your vision,

No one to talk to so I run to find someone who'll listen….

I don't know who I am, I'm lost I reckon

I'm having second thoughts because I'm always thought of second......

Running to where I'm supposed to be like Tetris,

Hoping to one day get a good start, like breakfast

Running from the world and running from crime,

Pork isn't good for you so I'm running from swine,

Searching for Benjamin's and running from dimes,

There's not enough hours in the day so I'm running from time.....

Running from death because of Heaven, I don't know if I'll get in,

So now I run to the Threshing Floor, the place where I get fed in,

But the Spirit gets quenched by interruptions I let in,

Now I need to *sprint* to Jesus before I run into a dead end......

Poison

Street fighting the night to get through the day,

Wrestling with my tongue to find the right words to say…..

…..To stay safe…….

Avoiding lies in disguise,

But they're so distinct, I see me in your eyes…..

Agitated and aggravated at the fact of being hated,

I cleverly get revenge without being deactivated,

Leaking out my own lies and letting them be evaporated,

They quickly dry up like blood coagulated.

I made this all up like it's fabricated,

Searching for this cure makes me feel free like
emancipated.

Fortunately, that doesn't make me any less a guy,

And it certainly leaves certain doubts rectified....

Yearning to be alone, but longing to be recognized

Searching for an antidote because I spit pesticide

Poison, created in the form of nonsense

The cure is, of course, obtaining common sense

Role Model

Being a human being, scheming to find a meaning

On this place we call Earth, dreaming for you to see me.

Getting cussed out, taking beatings just to be thee,

Not realizing there's little ones seeing me, trying to be
me……

Trying to interpret the perfect verse and splurge without
cursing,

It's worth the work because dirt hurts the parents that
birthed them,

The words reversed are murmured back to me, making
me vermin,

Conversely, verbs take action, that's what I'm taking, it's
urgent….

......That we send these kids the right message,

Especially for me because that means I was taught the right lesson.

To pass on knowledge and good deeds is a blessing,

For a black teen in this world full of stress and depression.

To top it all off like dressing,

Our focus should be
I.R.A.Q. where Ignorance Raises Abnormal Questions

As long as our troops stay there, Barack Obama would be the perfect role model as the 1st Black President.......

............Thanks Bush!

I Can't Take It

~I'm not trying to go back to the "night-light" days,
where I was scared my family wasn't gonna make it......

......That's why I'm trying to get my life Rite like Aid, so
I can take care of us because I can't take it.........

-You ever woke up in the night and heard your mama
crying?

She told you she was sick but you knew she was lying....

She's struggling to pay and get you what you want, and
she's trying to do it all by herself; now you feel like
dying.....

You think it's your fault she has a life but can't live it,

Now you're messed up like the stomach flu on
Thanksgiving,

You wish there was money in the bank, hidden

But there's none so thoughts of suicide arise, I ain't
kiddin'

She'll save money with you gone, but then she'll be all alone

She's already depressed and stress is accident-prone.

You're trapped like one man in a 2-3 zone,

The thought is so overwhelming, you feel it in your bones….

Plus you want to go to Heaven, so suicide isn't logical,

Then, what if you try it and fail? Now she has MORE bills from the hospital

She always told me failure isn't an option as loud as success is possible.

~I'm not trying to go back to the "night-light" days, where I was scared my family wasn't gonna make it……

……That's why I'm trying to get my life Rite like Aid, so I can take care of us because I can't take it………

-People don't agree with the ways that their peers of today

Get money to survive, it's drug money in their eyes.

They figure you can hustle without killing or telling lies,

Which is true but us Blacks don't think that way…..

Worried about buying Fitteds with your new Jays,

Worried about Girbaud and some new Bapes,

And wonder why every 5 minutes, someone gets shot for their Yays,

That's how us Blacks think today….

Ready to lynch Kramer for calling us the N-word

Yet Black comedians say it and we don't find it absurd…..

Blind, deaf, and mute, stuck with tunnel vision,

Keeping on the lights and gas is not the main mission….

Rushing home from work to watch games by the Pistons,

But your kids are starving, there's no food in the Kitchen!

I'm pulling my hair out, and going bald like Krillin,

Because these Androids are in my way of "Taking off These Limits"

……..I can't take it anymore…..

Road Rage

Mobilized on this path of solid concrete, my mind is in a maze

I'm hunting and craving to see the end of this daze like a flash grenade

My mind is a Street Fighter, boxing with desires, conserving sonic booms like Guile

All the while my thoughts conquer them both, turning my body Cold like Case Files

Freezer burn, brain freeze

Avalanche, arctic breeze

My mind is undergoing a physical change

Because it can be changed back with the rage and the range that the Rays of the Sun always sustain

Do I want to heat up or cool off?

This fork in the road is inevitable because apparently

My destiny is manifested by scrutiny

So I can't see clear like transparencies

Hoping and praying, eagerly awaiting, for the millisecond I make my decision

Go left to the heater, or right to the freezer, a lesson can be learned from each mission

To prolong this, like distance

And sweeten life, like berries

 I sort of feel oBliged like Mary

To keep straight and let loose all my components

So I can one day be on top like exponents..........

Pressure

(This is dedicated to my K.P. fam!)

Pressure #1 (Bully)

Bad attitude, a confident swagger in my step

Taking nothing from no one, add a little extra pep

To increase my rep, I'm trying to be known

So people can fear and look up to me, I'm guessing I'm grown

Upholding this name is hard but I'm up to the challenge.

Willing to drop anyone who'll step up to the challenge

It's hard sometimes because I'm trying to get out of this,

but I got to be a leader in this mug because I don't follow kids.

Pressure from your peers is tough, even for bullies

Actually, it's harder for them to act rationally

Like if someone bumps me, they think that naturally

They're going to get beat down when I don't want to do it, fully.

Everyone's egging me on to stuff him in a locker

But that'll be my third strike and I'll get kicked out like soccer

The boy didn't mean it, actually he's kind of cool

But at school, the pressure's on, and I still got to cruel.

I'm going to late for a class I planned to skip because I didn't do my homework

This being good thing won't work…..

He has the work and could probably help me

If I asked him for it now, I'd have a friendship that's healthy

What to do? If I don't they'll probably use me like a tool

Do I want my name or a friend that likes me because I'm cool

I let the pressure get me, forget about the rules

Just got the third strike and now I got to find another school

………....Pressure………

Pressure #2 (Bad Boys)

I'm all by myself, a leader who I follow

Messed up in the past, so make up for it tomorrow

Wait…..………..what if there isn't one?

Now I have to hurry…..

Because I don't want to be clouded by little things like flurries

My judgment can be clouded by things running in my mind,

Like I want to beat up that nerd and take his girl because she fine….

In that, the pressure of sex arises, but I simply can't,

Because I'm a Christian that don't feel like having to repent

My boys are like "Forget about her and let's go get blowed."

Before I knew it my mouth said "Yea" but my mind's like NO!

In the car, passin' and puffin', laughin' and cussin', acting a fool,

Mid afternoon, taking a cruise, knowing that we should all be in school….

Cops pulled up behind us, sirens screaming and crying

We yelled "5-0!"

but Jay's too high, he thinks we're lying…

"I ain't goin to jail for nobody", said 12 year old Brian.

And for a second I blacked out as he pulled out a 9 and….

Shot!

At Jay, kicked him out, and hopped in the driver seat

I grew up with little dude but never thought twice I'd die with him

Of course we got caught, and like Oreo's I was smack-dab in the middle

Feeling like the opposite of a giggle

High for the first time, seeing shots for the first time

Can blame no one but myself, should've followed my first mind

Instead of going to school I became a headline

Trying to fit in with some clowns, now the center of a crime………..

…………Pressure………..

Pressure #3 (Wrong Turn)

A mother and a daughter just began to have a heated conversation.

The daughter told her mom, "I'm losing my concentration.

I missed my period and I don't mean the punctuation."

She started crying because her mother got quiet and started pacing….

"Girl what are you talking about? What were you thinking?"

"I'm sorry Mama, me and this boy, we got to drinking at this party then he asked me could he take me for a ride…

…..I said yes because he seemed like a nice guy……

There must've been something in my drink he must've mixed in,

because the next thing I knew we were in this room kissing.

I tried to get out of it but he wouldn't listen

Then he relaxed and relieved me of all my tension……"

All of a sudden it got quiet like detention.

Mom's not ready for sex and daughter to be in a sentence…..

They sat quietly, contemplating their next move,

The mom was now searching for the right words to choose….

She wanted to understand but couldn't help being logical

So she asked, "Why you have to be so irresponsible?

Letting any and everybody come on to you!

Why are two simple letters these days so impossible?

Going to parties and getting drunk, have you gone crazy?"

"Mom, I'm gone be sixteen with a newborn baby!

I don't want it to come it asking "who's gone raise me?"

Now I messed up but dang now you gone blaze me!?"

She stormed out the room now more lost and confused

"Just last week man, I could be the boss of the room

Now my package has been opened up, tossed and misused

My life is just another story now lost in the news.....

I was at my life's subject, now I'm at the predicate,

because I'm not a DVD, Definitely Very Delicate.

Time passes very quick,

with not much evidence.

Now my only way out seems very prevalent…..

Time is against me so I'm not going to take up

anymore space like leaves that need to be raked up."

With that she went in the bathroom

       combed her hair

          and put on makeup

Took a bottle of pills

and went to sleep……

………..never again to wake up…….

………..Pressure……..

Inspirational

Eyes

When you look at me, what do you see?

Do you see adolescence, or do you see maturity?

Do you see disgust, or do you see pleasantry?

Do you see demise, or do you see life abundantly?

Well, I stand before you as a man of many mistakes.

I've correctly used my brain enough to fill up a milk
crate,

And as I watch my thoughtlessness seep through those
holes,

My adolescence seemed to allow me to dig deeper like a
mole.

Again, when you look at me, what do you see?

Do you see humility, or do you see conceit?

Do you see honesty, or do you see deceit?

Do you see strength, or do you see frailty?

You see the thing that I have come to realize,

Is the fact that life *is* a prize……..

….It's a gift that we've won based on God's grace,

But even still some only see with their eyes and not their faith.

So, when you look at me, what do you see?

Do you see 2 Timothy 3:2-5, or Galatians 5:22-23?

Do you see me in need of God, or do you see God in me?

In essence, yes, God is in me, *and* I constantly need Him.

So while I may not give a bum all my money, I will feed him

But intending to be fruitful, hungry for Him in my stride,

I have taken the hearts of others for a joyride

But more important than how you see me, how do you see you?

I've made mistakes and repented for what I did and used to do

But repenting is no good if I keep going back....

Knowing that, are *we* wasteful or frugal.........?

In the eyes of this man that stands sockless in the sand,

I can admit that I've taken a heart and had it canned

In remorse and retribution of that heart,

I've vowed to grow strong and mature as God's partisan

In order for you to see you, I must correctly see me

My past can no longer be a hindrance to my self-esteem

We must *all* move forward, and *all* become redeemed

Work on one accord on this Earth as a Dream Team

Now that we've all seen each other, it's my full intent

To encourage you to seek ye the Lord and repent

I'm not the best example, better yet the opposite, like the Secant

But it's not me who you come to at the Day of Judgment....

As we await His return, I have one final question......

.........*How does He see you*...........*?*

Speaking Out

No pen, no paper, there's no reason for writing……..

No tissue, no sniffles, there's no reason for crying……..

All truth, no fibs, there's no reason for lying……..

All faith, all hope, there's no reason for dying……..

………… And going to hell………..

Black men have accepted crime as an excuse to fail

They've taken the bate and still haven't made bail

Then their mothers don't cry, they wail…..

So I've decided to be that bridge over life's troublesome
waters,

I'm going to be the help to the father-raped daughters,

I'm going to be the escape route from the stalkers,

AND BE IN CHARGE OF HELPING TO DEFEAT
THE ENEMY LIKE MANSLAUGHTER!!

It has slaughtered us, so we'll return the favor

But there's only one way, and that's through the Savior

I'm a newly Free Man, like Morgan Freeman

God has appointed me to help set us free man

We must now rebuke demons, and enter into repentance

SEND SATAN TO PRISON WITH AN ETERNAL
SENTENCE!!!!

DON'T BE IGNORANT, AND DON'T BE
ASHAMED

PLEASE FREE YOUR MIND, LIKE THE MATRIX,
DON'T BE AFRAID

Yes, I've done some things that I'm not proud to tell……….

But I've put them in God's hands and sent them out to Hell!

There's no application fee for God's glory,

I pray someone receives this, I hope you hear me…….

Genuine Worship

(To my Family in Christ)

I'm speaking life into dry bones,

> letting bygones be bygones,

> With hopes that God will sweep you off your feet
> like a cyclone

Yea Satan slithers into life, like a python

> But we have the power to evade him!

> Not degrade or erase him, just deflate him,

> So he can keep making tests and we can take
them,

> And Ace them!

Holy A.C.T.

> -Allow Christ to Touch

But first display to Him how much

We think the Most High is worthy of delivering
scholarship blessings

He needs to know we lean on Him like a crutch

Show these rocks who is Boss! Cry out in worship!

I tell you it's worth it, because it's our purpose

And He deserves it, so let your 1st wind,

Be a "Hallelujah!" and a "Thank You Jesus!"

I'll take this opportunity to state my thesis

"Where would I be without my Jesus!?"

I was created to make your name glorious

You died on the cross, rose, and now stand victorious

Seated at His Right Hand on the Throne

I love you Jesus and can't wait to come home

I know I must first fulfill Your requirements on Earth

So I'll seek you personally and find your true worth

My prayer life must increase, I must seek Your Holy Spirit

That is Your greatest gift to man, THANK YOU FOR YOUR HOLY SPIRIT!!!!

Once spiritually illiterate, because I was ignorant, and wasn't familiar with You

Now I feel it's significant, to become intimate, and strengthen my relationship with You

I comprehend Your choice to provide all kinds of weather

To show through it all, Your mercy endureth forever

O HOW I WORSHIP THEE,

ALL HAIL THE KING!

I'LL SPRAY WATER TOWARDS HEAVEN

AND HOPE YOU'LL POUR OUT SOME BLESSINGS!

I LOVE YOU!

Question of Faith

Have you ever felt like you're presently moving towards the future, away from the past?

Trying to get towards the front, away from the back….?

Trying to get to the beginning, away from the last…?

…And you still fall short, head down, feeling bad…….

…….It's called life…….

A lesson most people have yet to learn,

      Beggars begging for money they have to earn,

      Black folks with lifestyles they have yet to turn,

      Desires like flameless fires that are yet to burn.

That's when the Power of Prayer and Faith coincide

Because all are welcome to church but no one truly goes inside,

Especially those with problems, and those with pride,

Those that murder, and steal, and even those that lie,

That's why those that go in the light try to help those that hide,

Those that are afraid and even those that cry,

Those with spirits and superstitions seem to need it more,

Because some only by Honda to feel on one Accord with the Lord…..

There's a battle with Good and Evil,

A battle with Pride and Humble,

A battle with those that Hold On and those that Fumble,

For everything that makes you walk, there's something to make you stumble….

For everything that makes you walk there's something to make you crumble….

Don't let that crack your spirit, don't let that steal your joy,

Don't let it depress you, and don't let it take your voice,

You shouldn't question your faith and you have no choice,

To praise God the one that helps deaf-mutes make noise

And there's a lot a issues with us teens today,

We argue and say things we don't mean to say,

Instead of getting things to read, we play

And there's even a select few who drink and smoke weed today…..

….Yea, I said it….

But you people disagree with this topic, so I'll stop it,

Flip it, and provide you with knowledge so that you profit

Or pocket any, all, or a few words that I speak

I'm confident you will although it's confidence I seek….

And not just me, but we as teens,

Don't fear others, but fear ourselves, no self-esteem

Starving for it, so hungry that when we get it we get greedy

Thinking we're the world's 8th Wonder like Stevie

Don't put yourself before others, but after God

Because He gave you a brain to think you're the cream of the crop

You're not invincible!

(scoff) Please, it was Jesus that stopped,

Anything from hurting you, so I believe that you're not!

Yea you're struggling to meet ends while your kids are in trouble,

Yea you wish you were in a Jacuzzi full of bubbles,

And I know that every time you dry off you step in a puddle,

But you still have to keep the faith and know that He loves you……

Your dedication and consecration will lead to the manifestation of all the blessings that you've been waiting for!

You can't just be a Sunday Christian, praise Him everyday, what kind of fool do you take Him for!?

I know the devil is a liar and he makes you so mad, so mad, that you just hate him more!

But if you think about it, life is full of choices, so if you made those decisions, what you blame him for......?

Just do the right thing and learn from your mistakes instead of altering your whole lifestyle, what are you changing for?

Also, look to the future, like right now, what are you hanging to my last statement for!!?

I know some are saying, "Who is this 16 year old giving me advice, who is he mistaken for?"

Well, I'm not ashamed to say that I'm a child of God and I'm trying to give ya'll another reason to praise Him for!!

On my part, that job would be useless unless Jesus Christ is who you truly have a craving for!!

If so, don't prepare to leave because we're practicing for Heaven so you may as well stay for more!!

If you're staying, please prepare to blatantly shout and act a fool until your face is sore!!!!!

So you can be a display to the world that when blessings come down instead of making them rain, they pour!!

Breaking Point

At this point in my life I have so much on my mind,

I don't even know what to put in my lines.

I'm tired of having cabinets with nothing to eat in it,

or walking through hallways with the smell of chief in it.

I wish I could just be myself and think,

because I feel like my Titanic has begun to sink.

Just trying to stay calm, trying to hold my composure,

because I don't want to be a man struggling to stay sober.

I hate the feeling of having to look over my shoulder,

like a wife whose husband left but keeps on trying to come over.

All in one week I feel like I've been crushed by a boulder,

and this world is so backwards that global warming feels colder…

People don't want to be near me, and I don't want to be people,

so I hope you hear me before I crash like Don Cheadle.

The Warriors got to the Playoffs, the Cavs are playing defense,

God is coming soon and people still don't choose to repent,

Was with a girl, but not the one she wanted to be with,

And I'm not a deodorant so why keep it a secret!?

Let me cut that branch off while I'm still at the stem,

Before I start making songs like Eminem did Kim…

I think I've finally reached my breaking point

At the moment I'm struggling to stay on point

Mind boggled; walking in circles I'm feeling weak,

Tired of jumping through hoops and hurdles while feeling bleak.

And every moment there's someone dying for something new,

while others have so much that they don't know what to do.

Then you got the people that blame Bush and the white man

When yes it's mostly their fault, but the rest is your life, man….

I'm tired of beggars at gas stations and red lights,

I'm tired of seeing little kids that haven't been fed right,

I sound like the people that actually want to do something

While there's plenty that can but won't do nothing……

…..Then they wonder they aren't successful and millionaires

Because they got stupid names like Chamillionaire…

Papers stacked up, they in living room, bills in air

Then they "Set It Off" and end up killed somewhere

They walk around, eyes dilated, drug abusing

The amusement really comes when you see dice shooting

The problem really comes when they get to shooting

That's why this is my life's first chapter and their life's conclusion

Every decade, man, there's something different

Racism, gangs, now war, dang, what's the difference….

I know you're probably going to laugh

Because you just got a new car, so you're going to laugh

Mama keeps telling you that you're going to pass

Because she doesn't want you living under the freeway overpass

I'm different from other people that you've met before

That's why this is filled with the truth and not metaphors

Kids have seen Techs before, even met some whores

And wonder why they're stuffed with more food than
Deca Stores!

Meanwhile these fat kids are just too greedy lend a

Few bucks to those poor, starving kids in Kenya

Some people blame themselves, others blame Bush,

They all blame each other and just beat around the bush

They just need a little push, along with some guidance

Because you can't have a car, if you're scared to drive it

So drive slow-

-But that don't mean cruise or ride low

Especially if you can't see or got to wear bifo-cals,

And people be killing me with these cars

These 4.0 gangsters and nerds that act hard

Finally, I got over 60 bars/

While some quarterbacks can't throw 60 yards

To get to the North, Africans used over 60 stars

Put the three 6's together and get.......Three 6 Mafia!!

Come on man!

For everybody this should be a lesson

The devil's a liar; God gives you your blessings

As a matter of fact, I'm about to roll this up like a seven

And try to make a difference so I can get into heaven

~1~

Printed in the United States
108538LV00004B/43-57/A

9 780980 129793